The KnowHow Book of Action Games

Usborne Publishing

Written and devised by:
Anne Civardi

Contributors:
James Opie, Andras Ranki
and Christopher Carey

Designed by:
John Jamieson
Illustrated by:
Malcolm English

First published in 1975
Usborne Publishing Ltd
20 Garrick Street
London WC2E 9BJ

Printed in Great Britain by
W S Cowell Ltd
Ipswich

About This Book

This book shows you how to make and play lots of different kinds of games. There are board games, dice games, table games, races, battle games, paper games and puzzles. Most of the games are made from things you can probably find at home. There is a list on page 4 which tells you what things you need and where to get them.

At the end of the book there are six pages of party games, party races and treasure hunts.

The measurements given are only a guide. You can make the games any size you like.

Remember to read the rules of each game carefully so you understand how to play them before you begin.

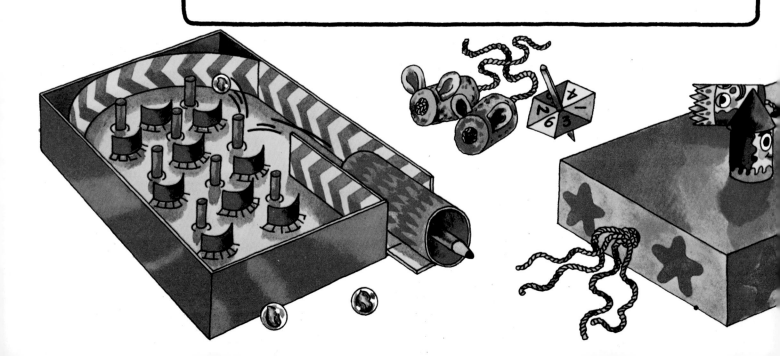

The KnowHow Book of Action Games

Contents

Getting Ready

These are the things you need to make the games in this book:

Thick cardboard – cut from strong cardboard boxes which you can get in supermarkets.
Thin cardboard – cut from empty cereal packets, backs of writing pads, or document folders which you can buy in stationery shops.
Glue – use Bostik 1 or UHU.
Sheet sponge – artificial sponge sold in sheets in Woolworth's and department stores.
Plasticine – sold in toy shops.
Tiddly wink counters – flat, round plastic counters sold in packets in toy shops.
Draught counters – wooden or plastic counters used to play draughts and sold in toy shops.
Dowelling rods – wooden sticks sold in hardware shops.
Garden canes – buy in gardening shops or florists'.
Eye screws – buy in hardware stores.
Paint – use poster paint or water colours.
Tracing paper – use greaseproof paper or very thin, see-through paper.

Ask your friends to help you collect things like:
Plastic and cardboard cartons, such as empty yoghurt, cream and cheese pots.
Cardboard tubes – from kitchen and lavatory rolls.
Cardboard or plastic egg boxes.
Bag ties – used to tie up freezer and garbage bags.
Cardboard boxes in lots of sizes.
Thin and thick cardboard.
Empty squeezy bottles.
Corks, empty matchboxes, hairpins, pipe cleaners, marbles and cardboard cheese boxes.

Home-made Boxes

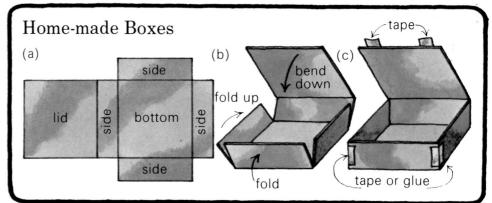

If you cannot find a box, make one out of cardboard. Use a ruler to draw the lines. The lid and bottom are the same size and the sides are all the same size (a).

Fold the cardboard, like this, to make the lid, bottom and sides (b). Stick the side and the bottom together with glue or tape (c). Try making a box without a lid.

1 Who Begins?

There are lots of ways to choose the starter of a game. One is for all the players to throw a dice. The one with the highest number starts (a). Play clockwise from the starter.

Another way is for one player to hold different length straws. Each player picks one. The one with the longest straw starts (b). Or cut up slips of paper. Draw an X on one.

4

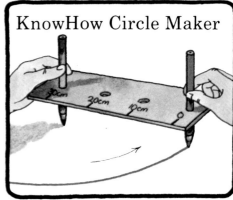

KnowHow Circle Maker

Measure and punch holes every 10 cm on a strip of thin cardboard, like this. Stick pencils through two holes. Holding both pencils firmly, swing one round in a circle.

Cardboard Dice

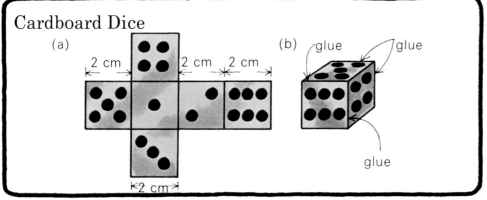

(a)

2 cm   2 cm   2 cm

2 cm

(b) glue   glue

glue

To make a cardboard dice, draw this shape, with all the sides 2 cm long, on some thin cardboard. Paint the dots in each square, like this (a).

Fold inwards along the lines and glue the sides and the top together (b). On bought dice the two sides opposite each other always add up to seven.

Plasticine and Sugar Dice

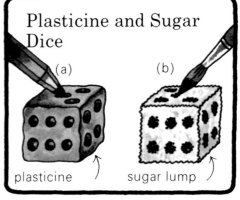

(a)   (b)

plasticine   sugar lump

To make a dice, shape a lump of plasticine into a cube and mark in the dots with a pencil point, like this (a). You can also ink dots on a sugar lump to make a dice (b).

(c)   (d)

Fold them in half and jumble them up. Everyone takes a slip. The player with the X starts (c). When there are only two players, toss a coin to see who starts (d).

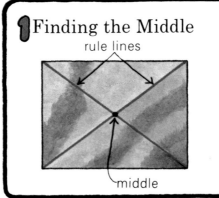

1 Finding the Middle

rule lines

middle

To find the middle of a box, a piece of cardboard or a sheet of paper, rule lines across it from the four corners, like this. The middle is where the lines cross.

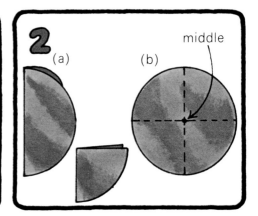

2

middle

(a)   (b)

To find the middle of a paper or thin cardboard circle, fold it in half twice, like this (a). Open the circle out again. The middle is where the two folds cross (b).

Beetle Bugs

(for 2 or more players)

Make enough Beetle Bug parts to build a complete Bug for each player. If you do not have any plasticine, try using clean potatoes for the head and body.

You will need
a dice and a yoghurt pot for a
  dice shaker

For each Beetle Bug
plasticine or 2 potatoes
a toothpick or matchstick and
  some silver foil
2 paper fasteners
thin wire (about 10 cm long)
tissue paper, a pencil and
  some strong glue
6 used matchsticks

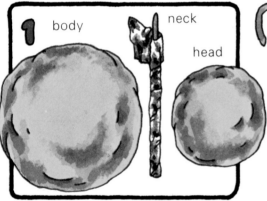

1 body   neck   head

Shape two lumps of plasticine into a round body and a smaller round head. Wrap silver foil round a toothpick or used matchstick to make the neck.

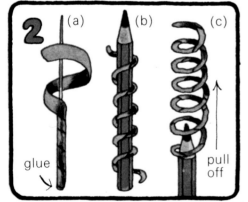

2 (a)   (b)   (c)

glue   pull off

To make a curly tongue, wrap a strip of tissue paper round the thin wire. Glue the paper at both ends **(a)**. Twist the wire round a pencil, like this **(b)**, and slide it off **(c)**.

How to Play

The idea is to build a complete Bug by throwing the dice for each part of the body. Each number on the dice matches a part of the body. If you throw a number you do not need, wait until your next turn.

To start, each player must throw a 1 for the body. Then throw a 2 for the neck or a 6 for each leg. When he has the neck, he throws for the head and the eyes and tongue. The winner is the first player to make up a Beetle Bug with a body, neck, a head, 2 eyes, a tongue and 6 legs.

Numbers to Throw

body	⚀
neck	⚁
head	⚂
eye	⚃
tongue	⚄
leg	⚅

Frog Leaps

(for 2 or more players)

This is a frog race. Each player needs a cardboard frog. The frogs start at one end of the strings and jump along to the other. The finishing line can be a mark on the floor or ponds made out of cardboard for the frogs to jump into.

You will need
thick cardboard
a piece of string (about 2 metres long) for each player
tracing paper
a pencil and some paint
scissors
thin cardboard to make the cardboard ponds

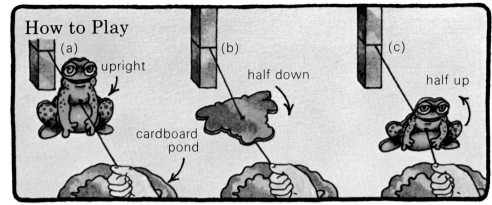

How to Play

Fasten one end of each string to a chair leg so the frogs stand in a line with their feet just touching the floor. Put a cardboard pond at the other end of each string.

Each player holds the end of a string and jerks it up and down to make the frog leap along it. The first frog to get into its pond or past the finishing line wins.

Trace this frog pattern on tracing paper **(a)**. Turn the paper over and scribble over the back **(b)**. Put it, right side up, on the cardboard and draw round the pattern again **(c)**.

Cut out the frog shape. Paint it a bright colour with big eyes and a mouth. Make a hole in the middle of the body where the mark is and thread string through it.

Frog Pattern

There and Back

(for 2, 3 or 4 players)

This is the great bicycle race all the way to Chiromo Village and back. Play the game on this board.

How to Play

Each player needs a cardboard bicycle, made as shown below. The first player to race his bicycle from the Cycle Park to Chiromo Village and back to the Cycle Park is the winner. Players take their cycles with them when they go by air or sea.

To start, each player puts his bicycle on one of the squares in the Cycle Park. Everyone throws the dice. The player with the highest number begins by moving his bicycle the number of points on the dice. When two bicycles land on the same square, those two players must shout, 'give way'. The last one to shout the words loses his next turn.

Players must take different routes from each other when they go by air or sea. Some routes are faster than others. The supersonic jet is faster than the balloon and the steamer is faster than the rowing boat.

Making the Bicycles

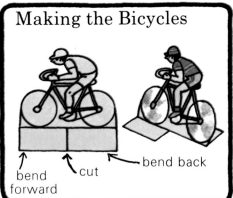

bend forward
cut
bend back

To make a bicycle, trace this pattern on to some cardboard and cut the shape out. Paint the bicycles a different colour for each player.

8

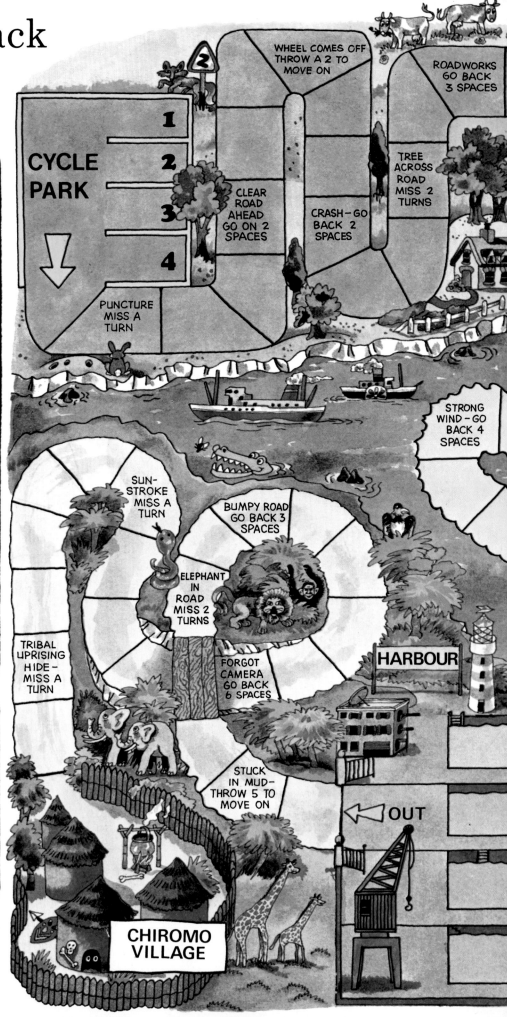

CYCLE PARK

1
2
3
4

WHEEL COMES OFF THROW A 2 TO MOVE ON

ROADWORKS GO BACK 3 SPACES

CLEAR ROAD AHEAD GO ON 2 SPACES

CRASH—GO BACK 2 SPACES

TREE ACROSS ROAD MISS 2 TURNS

PUNCTURE MISS A TURN

STRONG WIND—GO BACK 4 SPACES

SUN-STROKE MISS A TURN

BUMPY ROAD GO BACK 3 SPACES

ELEPHANT IN ROAD MISS 2 TURNS

TRIBAL UPRISING HIDE—MISS A TURN

FORGOT CAMERA GO BACK 6 SPACES

HARBOUR

STUCK IN MUD—THROW 5 TO MOVE ON

OUT

CHIROMO VILLAGE

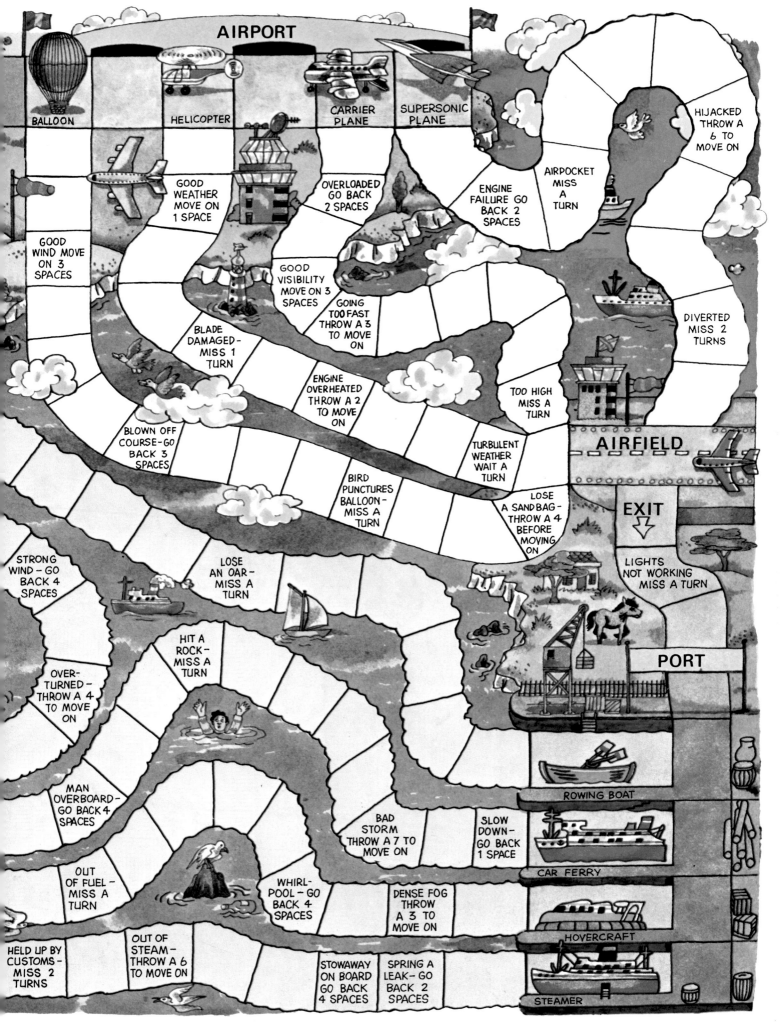

Looping the Loop

(for 2 or more players)

This is a target board. The further you stand from the board, the harder it is to get the rings round the pegs.

You will need
a big cardboard box lid (about 28 cm wide and 40 cm long)
coloured paper or paint
5 cardboard tubes cut from a kitchen roll, or thin cardboard
thick cardboard
strong glue and string
scissors and a pencil

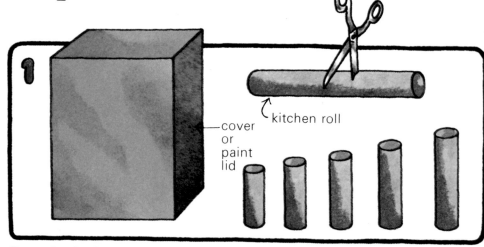

1 cover or paint lid — kitchen roll

To make the board, cover a cardboard box lid with coloured paper, or paint the outside and leave it to dry.

Make five cardboard pegs out of kitchen rolls, like this. The longest should be about 12 cm long and the shortest about 8 cm long, as shown.

4 glue

Glue the pegs, slanting upwards, to the outside of the lid. Put the shortest one in the middle and the others close to the four corners, like this.

5 paint

When the pegs are firmly stuck to the lid, paint them all different colours. Leave them to dry.

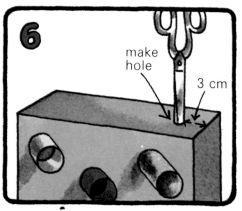

6 make hole — 3 cm

Turn the board on one side and make a hole about 3 cm from the top, like this. Do the same on the other side. Thread a piece of string through the holes. Knot the ends.

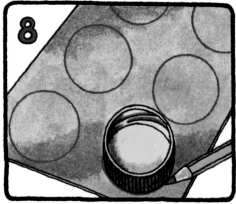

8

Draw ten circles on a sheet of thick cardboard, using the bottom of a tin or coffee jar lid as a guide. Make sure the circles are at least twice as wide as the pegs.

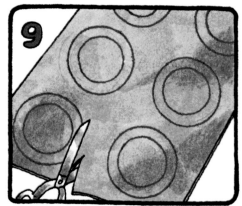

9

Using a slightly smaller lid or tin, draw a circle inside each big circle, like this. Cut round the big circles and then cut out the middle circles.

10 paint

Glue two circles together to make a thick cardboard ring. Do this to all the circles so that you have five rings. Paint each ring the same colour as one of the pegs.

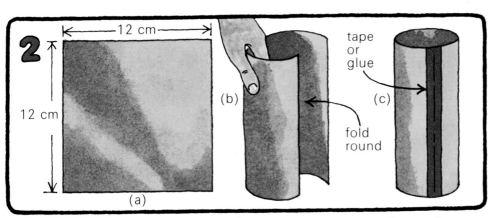

2 12 cm / 12 cm / (a) / (b) / fold round / tape or glue / (c)

If you do not have any old cardboard tubes, make the pegs out of thin cardboard. Cut five pieces of cardboard, each about 12 cm wide and 12 cm long (a).

Curl each piece round your finger (b) and tape or glue the two edges together (c). Cut them so they are all slightly different lengths.

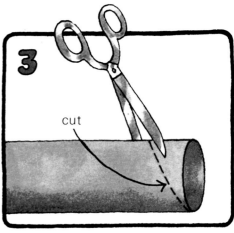

3 cut

Cut one end of each tube at an angle, like this. This is to make them slant upwards when you glue them on to the cardboard box lid.

7 2 / 5 / 10 / 4 / 1

Cut out five small squares of white paper. Glue one square below each of the coloured pegs. Draw or paint the numbers shown on the squares.

How to Play

Hang the board on a door. Draw a line on the floor about 2 metres from the board. Stand behind the line and try to throw the rings on to the pegs. Throw the five coloured rings in a turn.

If you step over the line while throwing, miss a turn. When a ring lands round a peg, score the number of points marked under the peg. If a ring lands round the same coloured peg, score twice the number. The first to score 50 points wins.

11

Five Minute Games

(for lots of players)

The games on these two pages are very easy to make and only take a few minutes to play.

You will need
For Egg Flip
2 cardboard egg boxes and a fork
For Catchball
2 tall plastic cartons
a ping pong ball
8 rubber bands
thin and thick cardboard
For Blow Football
2 small cardboard boxes
plasticine and 2 straws
a ping pong ball
For Ribbon Roll
1 tall, plastic carton
5 small yoghurt pots
ribbon (about 3 cm wide and 90 cm long)
a pin
thick cardboard and white paper
5 marbles
For Matchbox Bullseye
thin cardboard and a matchbox
For all the games
paint, glue, scissors, a pencil and sticky tape

1 Egg Flip

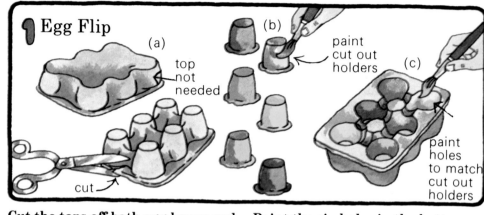

Cut the tops off both egg boxes and throw them away. Cut the six egg holders out of the bottom of one (a). Paint each egg holder a different colour (b). Leave to dry.

Paint the six holes in the bottom of the second egg box. Make them the same colours as the egg holders, like this (c).

2

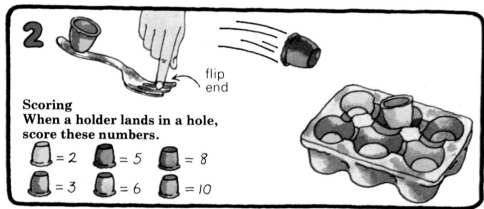

Scoring
When a holder lands in a hole, score these numbers.

$\bigcirc$ = 2 $\bigcirc$ = 5 $\bigcirc$ = 8
$\bigcirc$ = 3 $\bigcirc$ = 6 $\bigcirc$ = 10

Put the painted egg box bottom on the floor. Put a fork about 45 cm from the box, like this. To play, balance an egg holder, open end up, on the handle end of the fork.

Push down quickly on the prongs and try to flip the holder into a hole in the egg box. Mark down the score. A holder that lands in the same-coloured hole scores double.

1 Catchball

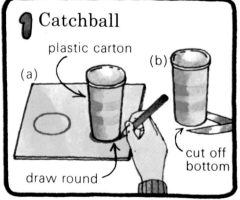

Draw two circles on cardboard, using the bottom of a plastic carton (a). Cut them out ½ cm smaller all the way round. Now cut off the bottom of the carton (b).

2

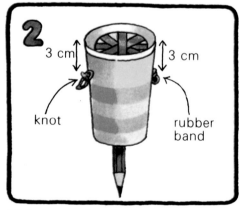

Make a catcher in the same way as you would make a cannon (see page 17). Instead of a cardboard tube, use the plastic carton and the circles you have cut out.

3

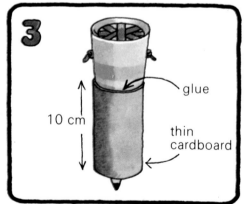

Cut out a strip of thin cardboard, about 23 cm wide and 10 cm long. Glue it round the bottom of the plastic carton catcher, like this. Now make another catcher.

12

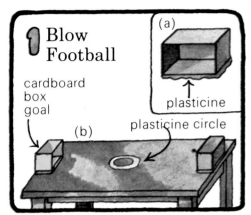

1 Blow Football

cardboard box goal

(a) plasticine

plasticine circle

(b)

Put some plasticine on the bottom of two small cardboard boxes (a). Push them, plasticine side down, on to the ends of a table (b). Put a plasticine circle in the middle (c).

2

Two people, or four people playing in teams of two, can play. To start, put a ping pong ball in the plasticine circle in the middle of the table, like this.

The players each have a straw and stand on either side of the table. The idea is to blow the ping pong ball, using the straws, into the other team's goal.

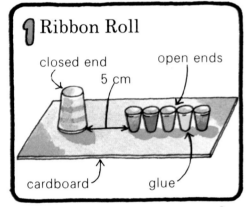

1 Ribbon Roll

closed end

5 cm

open ends

cardboard

glue

Glue five yoghurt pots, open ends up and touching each other, to cardboard. Glue a tall, plastic carton, open end down, about 5 cm from the first pot, like this.

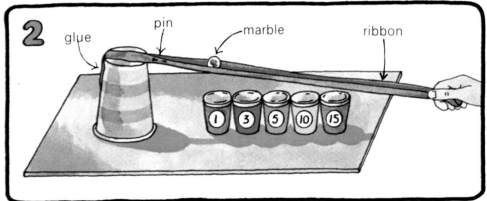

2

glue pin marble ribbon

1 3 5 10 15

Glue one end of some ribbon, about 3 cm wide and 90 cm long, to the top of the carton. Pin the ribbon together close to the carton, like this, so that it funnels.

Draw these numbers on bits of paper. Glue them on to the pots. Roll marbles, one by one, down the ribbon and try to get them into the pots. Roll five marbles in a turn.

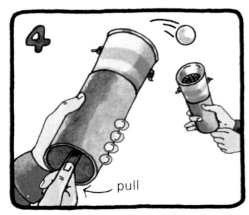

4

pull

Stand 3 metres apart and each hold a catcher. The game is to fire and catch a ping pong ball, using the catchers. The player to catch the ball five times in a row wins.

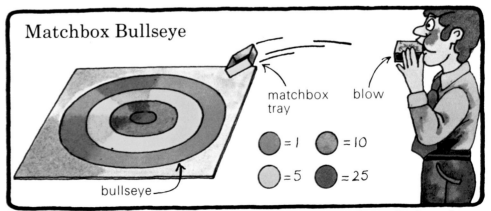

Matchbox Bullseye

matchbox tray

blow

= 1   = 10

= 5   = 25

bullseye

Draw a big circle on some cardboard. Draw three smaller circles inside it, like this. Paint them all different colours. When they are dry paint on the numbers.

Stand 3 metres from the board. Put a matchbox in your mouth and blow hard so that the match tray shoots out on to the coloured circles. Have three blows in a turn.

Mouse Trap

(for 3 or more players)

Each player needs a cork mouse. Instead of making a whirler you can play with a dice.

You will need
a cork for each player
pieces of string (each about 40 cm long)
a hairpin and felt cloth
scissors and strong glue
a big carton or little box
thin cardboard
a used matchstick or a toothpick
tracing paper and a pencil
paint and a paint brush
a circle of cardboard for the cardboard mat

1 Mouse Making

push down

Paint the corks different colours. Leave them to dry. Then make a hole through the middle of each cork, using closed scissors or a knitting needle, like this.

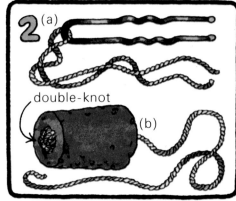

2 (a)

double-knot

(b)

Loop string, about 40 cm long, round a hairpin (a). Push the hairpin through the hole in a cork and double-knot the end of the string (b). Do the same to all the corks.

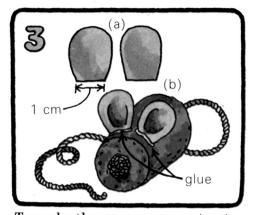

3 (a)

(b)

1 cm

glue

To make the mouse ears, cut out two pieces of felt this shape (a). Glue them to the top of the cork, like this (b). Put two ears on all the cork mice.

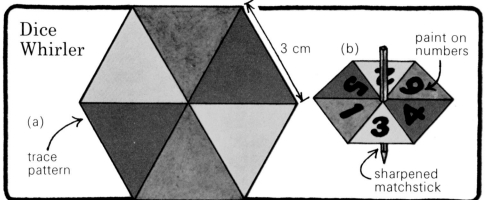

Dice Whirler

3 cm

(a)
trace pattern

(b)
paint on numbers

sharpened matchstick

Trace this pattern (a) on to thin cardboard. Rule lines from corner to corner, like this. Cut the shape out very carefully.

Paint the triangles and paint on the numbers. Sharpen a used match with a pencil sharpener. Push it through the middle of the whirler, where all the lines meet.

How to Play

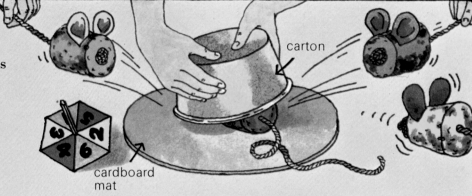

carton

cardboard mat

Players spin the whirler in turn. The one with the highest number is the mouse trapper. The others are the mouse holders. Each holder puts his mouse on the cardboard mat and holds its tail. The trapper spins the whirler. When it stops on a 6 or 4 he tries to trap the mice under the carton. The holders try to pull them away before being trapped. If the trapper catches a mouse he scores 5 points. A holder scores 5 points if he pulls his mouse away in time.

A holder loses 5 points if he pulls his mouse away when the whirler stops on a number other than a 6 or 4. The first player to score 50 points wins.

When the trapper has spun a 6 or 4 three times, he passes the carton to the player on his left who then becomes the new mouse trapper.

Fish Hook

(for 2 or more players)

This is a race against time. Try to hook as many cork fish as you can before all the salt runs out of the timer.

You will need
6 corks
6 eye screws or hairpins
some felt cloth
strong glue and white paper
a stick (about 50 cm long)
string
a hairpin or thin wire
scissors and paint
a plastic squeezy bottle
a glass jar
salt or fine sand

How to Play

Put the fish, screw ends up, on the floor. Take it in turns to hook the fish with the rod. Add up the numbers on the fish you have hooked after each turn.

A turn lasts as long as it takes for the salt to pour out of the squeezy bottle, once the lid has been opened. The first player to score 20 points wins.

1 Fish Making

Paint six corks different colours. Screw an eye screw into the middle of each cork, or push a hairpin into the cork, like this.

2

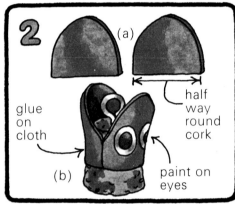

Cut two pieces of felt, each wide enough to wrap half-way round a cork (a). Glue the felt on to the cork and paint on eyes, like this (b). Do the same to all six corks.

3

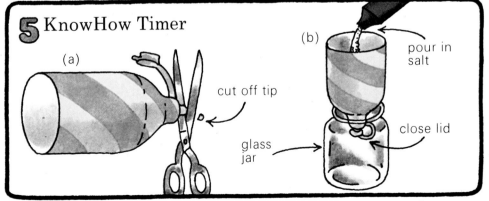

Cut out six pieces of white paper and glue one to the bottom of each cork. Paint numbers from one to six on the corks, like this.

4

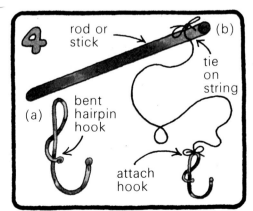

Tie string, about 58 cm long, to one end of a stick or rod. Bend a hairpin or some wire into a hook, like this (a) and tie it on to the end of the string (b).

5 KnowHow Timer

Cut a squeezy bottle in half. Cut off the very tip of the bottle, like this (a). Paint the bottle with brightly coloured paint. Leave it to dry.

Close the lid and balance the squeezy bottle, upside down, in a glass jar. Fill the bottle with salt or fine sand (b), making sure there are no lumps in it.

Cannonboard
(for 2 or more players)

The further you pull the pencil out of the cannon, the faster the marbles will go. Pull it very gently to get marbles into the goals nearest the cannon.

You will need

a strong cardboard box (about 34 cm wide and 46 cm long)
a sheet of thin cardboard
a strong cardboard tube (about 14 cm long)
4 rubber bands
6 marbles
sticky tape and strong glue
a pencil, a ruler and scissors

How to Play

Fire the marbles out of the cannon and try to get them into the goals with the high numbers. Each player fires six marbles in a turn. At the end of each turn add up the plus scores and take away the minus scores. The first player to score 100 points wins.

To fire, put one marble at a time into the top of the cannon. Pull back the pencil and then let it go.

1 The Board

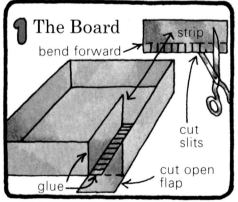

Cut a flap, about 6 cm wide, at one corner of the box. Cut a strip of cardboard half the length of the box and as high. Cut slits on one side. Glue the strip to the box.

2

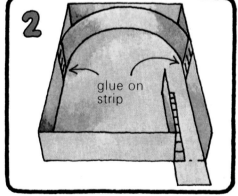

Cut a strip of carboard about 1½ times the width of the box and as high. Cut slits at both ends. Bend the strip into a half-circle and glue it to the sides of the box.

3

To make the goals, cut 13 pieces of cardboard, about 8 cm long and 3 cm wide. Cut slits at one edge of each piece. Bend them into half-circles. Glue them on to the box.

4

bend

(a)

4 cm

(b)

← 3 cm →

glue

Cut out eight strips of cardboard, about 4 cm x 3 cm. Cut slits along the edge of each strip, like this (a). Roll them into small posts and glue them, as shown (b).

Now glue the posts on to the box, like this. They are hazards and make the game a bit harder to play. Draw or paint the plus and minus numbers inside each goal.

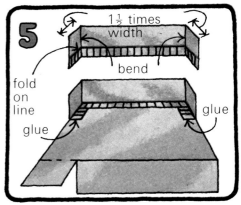

5

1½ times width

bend

fold on line

glue

glue

Cut some cardboard about 1½ times the width of the box and about 6 cm high. Cut slits along the edge. Bend the cardboard on the red lines. Glue it to the back of the box.

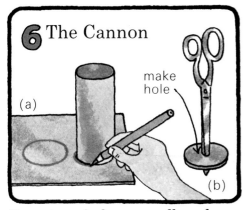

6 The Cannon

make hole

(a)

(b)

Draw two circles on cardboard, using the end of the cardboard tube. Cut them out, ½ cm smaller all the way round. Glue together. Make a hole in the middle.

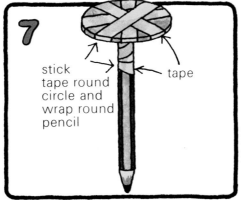

7

stick tape round circle and wrap round pencil

tape

Push the end of a pencil through the hole in the cardboard circle. Tape the circle on to the pencil very firmly, like this.

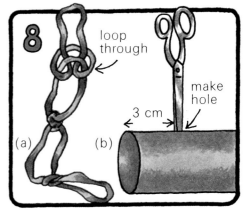

8

loop through

make hole

3 cm

(a)

(b)

Link four strong rubber bands together, like this (a). Make a hole on either side of the tube, about 3 cm from one end (b).

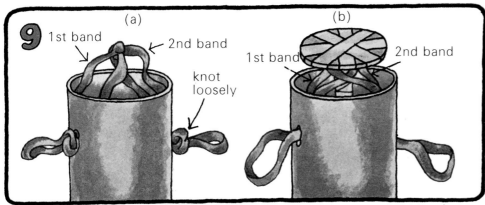

9

(a)

1st band

2nd band

knot loosely

(b)

1st band

2nd band

Thread the rubber bands through the holes in the cardboard tube, like this. Knot both ends very loosely (a).

Push the cardboard circle and pencil up the tube. First pull one rubber band over the circle and then the other, like this. Untie the loose knots (b).

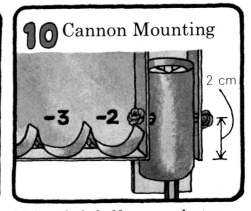

10 Cannon Mounting

-3 -2

2 cm

Make a hole half-way up the two bits of cardboard, about 2 cm from the open flap. Push the rubber band ends through the holes, like this. Double-knot each end.

Flick Billiards

(for 2 players or 2 teams)

To play this game, one player or team needs ten counters of one colour. The other player or team needs ten counters of a different colour. Glue a circle of paper to the top of an extra counter. We have used black and red counters.

You will need
a cardboard box with low sides
   (about 72 cm × 50 cm)
4 old nylon stockings
21 draught counters
a small yoghurt pot
thin cardboard
sticky tape and strong glue
scissors and a pencil

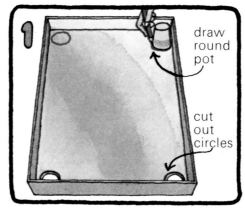

Draw a circle in each corner on the inside of the box, using a small yoghurt pot as a guide. Cut out the four circles.

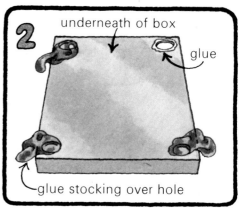

To make the corner nets, cut the feet off four old stockings. Glue one foot over each hole on the underneath of the box, like this.

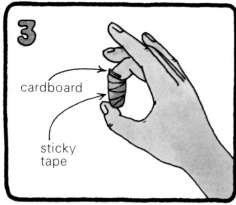

To make the finger guard, cut a strip of thin cardboard. Put it over the nail of your third finger. Wrap sticky tape round it, like this. The picture shows you how to flick.

How to Play

The player with the black counters starts. He flicks a black counter against a red one, trying to get the red one into a corner net. If he does, he has another turn. If not, the player with the red counters tries to flick a black one into a net. If either player flicks the extra counter into a net, he picks one of his counters and the extra one out of the net and puts them back on the board. The first one to flick all the other side's counters into the nets wins.

This picture shows how to set out the counters at the start of the game.

Tiddly Pong

(for 2 players)

This is just like ordinary ping pong except that you can play on a small table. Both players need a bat to hit the ball over the net to each other.

You will need
a sheet of thick cardboard
thin cardboard
a sheet of sponge
a saucer
an old nylon stocking
a ping pong ball
strong glue and sticky tape
scissors and string
a safety pin and 4 pencils

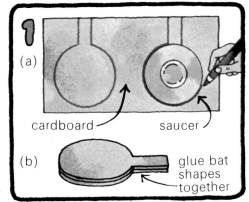

(a) cardboard saucer
(b) glue bat shapes together

Rule two lines, 4 cm apart and 10 cm long, on thick cardboard. Draw a circle at the bottom of the lines, using a saucer. Cut out the shapes. Glue them together. Do this again.

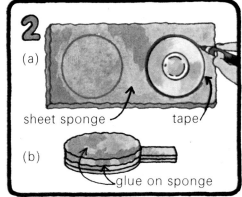

(a) sheet sponge tape
(b) glue on sponge

Using the same saucer, draw four circles on a sheet of sponge (a). Cut them out. Glue a sponge circle to both sides of a cardboard bat, like this (b).

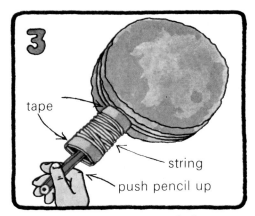

tape
string
push pencil up

Wrap string tightly round the handle of each bat. Glue the ends and wrap sticky tape round them. Push a pencil up the handles, between the two bits of cardboard.

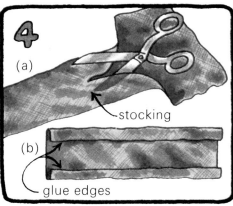

(a) stocking
(b) glue edges

To make the net, cut the foot off an old stocking. Cut open the stocking, like this (a). Fold over and glue about 2 cm at both edges, as shown (b).

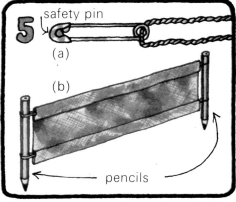

safety pin
(a)
(b)
pencils

Cut two bits of string 80 cm long. Loop them, one at a time, through a closed safety pin (a). Thread them through the folded stocking (b). Tie the ends to two pencils.

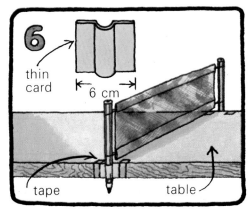

thin card
6 cm
tape   table

Cut two pieces of thin cardboard as long as the lip on the table you use and about 6 cm wide. Tape one to the middle of each side of the table. Push the pencils into them.

How to Play

The aim is to be the first to score 21 points. You score a point when the other player cannot return your shot. Take it in turn to serve.

Each player has 5 serves in a turn. The ball must bounce on both sides of the table when you serve. It must not bounce your side when you return a shot.

Sticks and Kicks

(for 2 players)

You will need

a strong cardboard box (about 48 cm long, 25 cm wide and 8 cm deep)

thick cardboard

a cardboard egg box

a strong cardboard tube (from a kitchen roll)

2 small string bags or a stocking

4 garden canes or 4 thin sticks (each about 60 cm long)

plasticine and 4 corks

4 big rubber bands

a pencil and paint

a small ball or large marble

How to Play

Put the box on a table. Put the ball or marble inside the circle on the centre line. Players stand on different sides of the table and hold a rod in each hand. Both start together.

The idea is to twist, push and pull the canes and try to get your footballers to kick the ball into the other team's goal. The first team to score three goals is the winner.

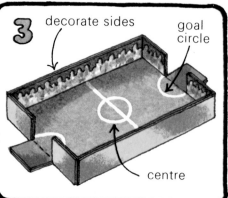

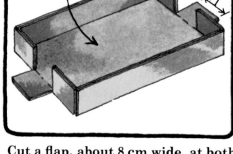

1 glue on strips / glue in cardboard

Cut some cardboard the size of the bottom of the box. Glue it inside the box, like this. Glue strips of cardboard to the sides and ends of the box, too.

2 paint / flap 8 cm wide

Cut a flap, about 8 cm wide, at both ends of the box, like this. Then paint the cardboard glued inside the box. Leave it to dry.

3 decorate sides / goal circle / centre

Draw a line across the middle of the inside of the box. Draw a circle on the line, like this, using a cup as a guide. Draw half-circles round the goal flaps.

20

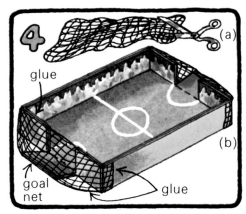

4 To make a goal net, cut open a string bag (a). Put one edge under the goal flap. Glue it underneath the box. Glue the other edge to the sides and top of the box (b).

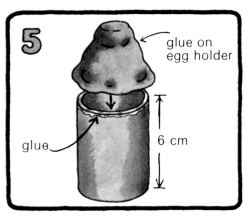

5 To make the footballers, cut the kitchen roll into six tubes, each 6 cm long. Cut the six egg holders out of the egg box. Glue one holder to the top of each tube.

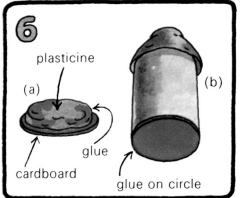

6 Draw round the bottom of each tube on cardboard. Cut out the circles. Glue plasticine to each one (a). Glue a circle, plasticine inside, to the bottom of each tube.

7 Paint faces on all the cardboard tubes. Paint three footballers one team colour and the other three a different team colour.

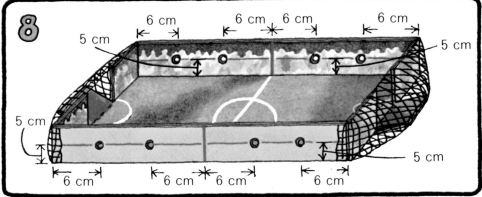

8 Measure the length of the sides of the box. Divide it in half to find the centre. Rule lines at the centre on both sides of the box, like this.

Make holes 6 cm from both sides of the centre lines and 5 cm from the bottom of the box. Make holes 6 cm from both ends and 5 cm from the bottom of the box, as shown.

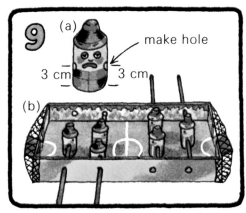

9 Push the canes through the holes in the box. Make holes in each tube (a). Push one team on to the canes at one end and the other team on to the canes at the other end (b).

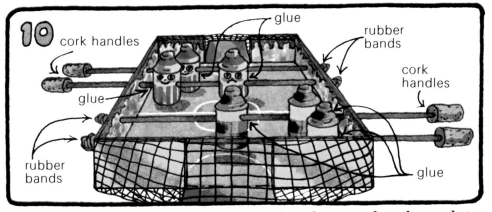

10 Push each cane through the second hole. Wrap a rubber band round the end of each cane, like this, to stop them from getting pulled back through the holes.

Push corks on to the other ends to make handles. Pull the rods so that the rubber bands are against the box sides. Then glue the footballers to the canes in position, like this.

Grand Derby

(for 2 or more players)

This is a horse race which you can play on any big table. Each player needs a horse and a jockey, and a piece of string long enough to loop round the table.

You will need
thin cardboard
tracing paper
a pencil and paint
string and scissors
strong glue
plasticine
wire bag ties, pipe cleaners or
    thin wire

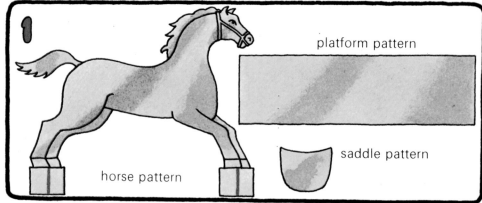

1

platform pattern

saddle pattern

horse pattern

To make a horse, draw the horse pattern, saddle pattern and platform pattern on tracing paper. Then trace the patterns on to some thin cardboard.

Cut the horse, saddle and platform shapes out of the cardboard. Cut along the red lines on the horse's feet. Paint the shapes and leave them to dry.

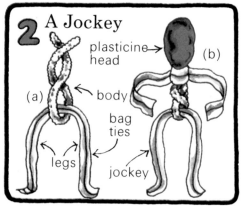

2 A Jockey

plasticine head

(a)

(b)

body

bag ties

legs

jockey

Twist two bag ties or bits of wire together for the legs and body (a). Twist another one round the body to make arms. Push a plasticine head on the body (b).

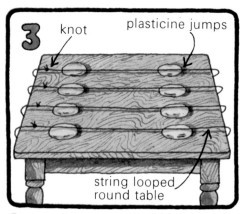

3

knot

plasticine jumps

string looped round table

Loop as many pieces of string as there are players round a table. Knot the ends. Press bits of plasticine down on the table under the strings, to make jumps.

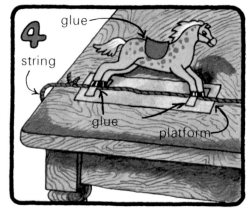

4

glue

string

glue

platform

Glue a saddle on to the back of each horse. Put a horse over each string. Pull the string up the slits on the horses' feet. Bend the slits, like this. Glue them to a platform.

How to Play

The game is to race your horse from one end of the table to the other without letting the jockey fall off. The horses must go over the jumps on the way. Anybody whose jockey falls off goes back to the beginning.

To start, put jockeys on the saddles. Line the horses at the start. Stand at that end of the table and pull the string under the table towards you. The first player to get his horse and jockey to the other end wins.

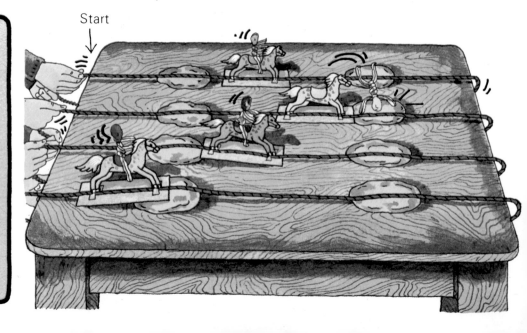

Start

Crossing the Line

(for 2 players)

Practise pushing the coin on to the board. Put it on the edge of the board and hit it with the palm of your hand so that it slides on to a coloured strip.

You will need
thick cardboard (about 30 cm wide and 32 cm long)
thin cardboard
a ruler and a pencil
cellophane and strong glue
paint and a paint brush
2 coins

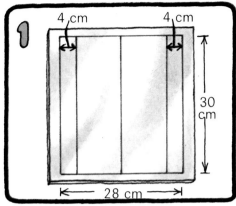

Draw a rectangle, 28 cm wide and 30 cm long, on a piece of thick cardboard. Rule lines down the middle of the rectangle and 4 cm from either side, like this.

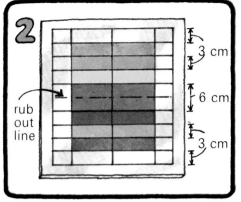

Rule nine lines, 3 cm apart, across the rectangle. Rub out the fifth line so that you have one 6 cm strip. Paint the seven middle strips different colours, like this.

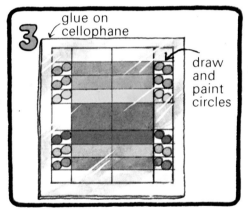

Draw two circles each side of the coloured strips, except the middle strip, using a small coin. Paint the circles the same colours as the strips. Cover with cellophane.

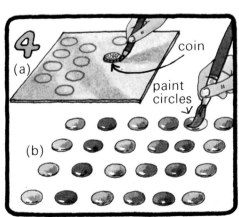

Using the same coin, draw 24 circles on thin cardboard (a). Cut them out. Paint four circles the same colour as each of the strips, except the middle strip (b).

How to Play

Put the board on a table. Lie a book behind it to keep it steady. Both players have a coin and 12 cardboard circles (2 of each colour). One person plays on the left half of the board, the other on the right half.

Start with the coins on the white strip closest to you. Take it in turn to push them on to the board. Each time the coin lands inside a coloured strip, cover one of the circles beside it with the same coloured cardboard circle. If it lands on a line, wait for your next turn. If the coin lands on the middle strip, miss your next turn. The first one to cover all 12 circles on his side wins.

23

2-In-1 Board

1. Matchmake
(for 2 or 3 players)

You will need
red, blue and green plasticine
used matches and drawing pins
a dice

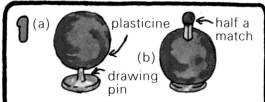

For the matchmen, push a small ball of plasticine on to a drawing pin **(a)**. Push half a match into the plasticine **(b)**. Make 14 red men, 14 blue men and 14 green men.

To set up the board, put the blue men on the dark blue squares, like this. Put the red men on the dark red squares and the green men on the dark green squares.

How to Play Matchmake

The game is to get your matchmen from the dark squares to the lighter squares of the same colour with stars. Each player has 14 men of one colour. Men can be moved in any direction except diagonally. Throw the dice to start. Then take turns.

Each turn move one man the number on the dice. You can capture an enemy man by landing on its square if it is not on its own colour. Take any captured men off the board and keep them. You cannot jump over men.

The game ends when one player has moved all his men still on the board on to his star squares. To score, each player counts his men on the star squares, adds the number of men he has captured and takes away his men not on star squares. The player with the highest score wins.

2. Hop Over (for 2 players)

You will need
12 green matchmen and 12 red
matchmen (see Matchmake)
1 dice

How to Play Hop Over

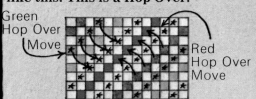

Red Home Row
Red Starting Row
Green Starting Row
Green Home Row

To start, put 4 green matchmen on
the pink star squares in the corner
of the board, like this. Put 4 red
matchmen on the red squares in the
opposite corner. One player moves
the green men, the other the red men.

The game is to get your 12 matchmen
from their Starting Row to their
Home Row. Throw the dice in turn.
Move one man each turn according
to the number you throw. You must
move a man if possible. Each time a
man is moved out of a Starting Row
square put on a new man. Take off
any man who reaches its Home Row.

Men can move sideways along the row
they are on but only in one direction
each turn. If they cannot go the full
distance, they cannot move. Men
can jump over their own men. Up
to 3 men can be on the same square.

A 6 on the dice can be used to move
any one man forward to its next row,
like this. This is a Hop Over.

Green Hop Over Move
Red Hop Over Move

A 5 may be used for a Hop Over from
a square with 2 or 3 men on it. A 4
may be used for a Hop Over from a
square with 3 men on it.

A man can only Hop Over one enemy
man if there are 2 or 3 men on the
square it is hopping from. A man can
Hop Over 2 enemy men if there are
3 men on the square it is hopping
from. The first player to get all 12 of
its matchmen Home wins. Or end
the game when 6 men reach Home.

Paper Games
(for lots of players)

Jumbled Newspapers

Each player has a jumbled up newspaper with the pages out of order, upside down and wrongly folded. Everyone starts together. The first player to put all the pages of his paper back into the right order wins.

Animals of Four

Players sit in a circle, each with a pencil and a slip of paper. They write the name of an animal across the top of the paper, fold it over so it cannot be seen and pass it to the player on their left. On the slip they have been passed they write the name of another animal, fold it over and pass it on. They do this four times. All the slips are put in the middle of the circle. Each player takes one. He draws a creature made up of the four animals written on his slip.

Noise Maker

One player is the noise maker. He collects ten things that make different noises. The other players each have a pencil and some paper. They sit in a room, close to a slightly open door. The noise maker stands behind the door. He shouts 'number one' and then makes his first noise by, perhaps breaking a hard biscuit.

The players write down what they think the noise is. The noise maker then shouts 'number two' and makes his next noise, perhaps rolling marbles round a tin. The players write down what they think it is. The player who has guessed the most noises right after the noise maker has made his ten noises wins.

Paper Hats

Each player has a big sheet of paper and some sticky tape. He has to make a hat out of the paper and put it on his head. The player who makes the best hat in three minutes wins.

Hangman

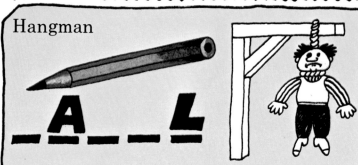

One player is the executioner. The other is the convict. The executioner thinks of a 6 or 7 letter word and marks down a dash for each letter on some paper. The convict tries to guess, one by one, the letters that make up the word.

For each wrong guess, the executioner draws in another part of the gallows and the hanging man. First the gallows, then the rope, then the head, the face, the body, the left arm, the right arm, the left leg and the right leg. If the convict guesses a letter in the word, the executioner writes it in position on the dash. If the convict guesses the whole word before he is hanged, he wins. If not, the executioner wins.

Team Drawing

One player is the boss. The others split into two teams. Each has some paper and a pencil. The boss writes down ten things to draw, such as 'tightrope walker', 'ringing telephone' or 'Olympics'.

The teams stand at opposite ends of the room with the boss in the middle. The first player in each team runs to the boss who tells them both to draw the first thing on his list. They run back and draw it in front of their teams. When the team has guessed what it is the second player runs to the boss for his drawing. The first team to guess all ten drawings wins.

Keep on Folding

Each player has one page of a newspaper. While music plays, everyone hops about. When it stops, everyone quickly folds their newspaper in half and stands on it. The last person to stand on his paper is out. The music starts again. When it stops the players fold their papers in half again and stand on them. This goes on until the papers have been folded into tiny squares and there is only one player left. He wins the game.

Drawing Blind

Players are blindfolded. Each has some paper and a pencil. They are told to draw a picture, such as a boat race, bit by bit. First they draw the sea, then the boats, then a lighthouse, the sky and the clouds. The blindfolds are taken off and the player who has drawn the best picture is given a prize.

Battleships

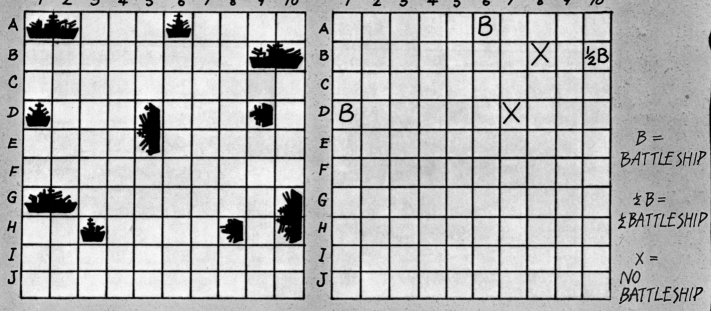

B =
BATTLESHIP

½ B =
½ BATTLESHIP

X =
NO
BATTLESHIP

This is a game for two. Both players draw two big squares on some paper and rule nine lines across and down them, as shown. Along the top of each big square they write numbers from 1 to 10. Down the side they write letters from A to J. One big square is the Battle Area, the other is the Target Area. Without letting each other see where, the players draw ten battleships on their Battle Areas. Five battleships cover two squares each and five cover one square each. The ships must not touch.

Players must not let each other see their papers during the game. They take it in turn to attack. Each turn a player calls out a number and a letter, such as A6. If the other player has a whole ship on that square, he says 'hit'. The attacker marks a B on his Target Area. If part of a ship is on that square, the defender says 'touched'. The attacker knows he has only sunk half a ship. If no ship is on that square, the attacker draws an X in the same square on his Target Area. Then the other player is the attacker. The winner is the first one to sink all the other player's battleships.

Push and Shove

(for 2 players or 2 teams)

For this board game, one player or team needs ten counters of one colour, the other needs ten of a different colour. The bigger you make the board, the more fun it is to play. Flick enemy counters off high scoring circles.

You will need

a big, square sheet of thick cardboard (about 64 cm long and 64 cm wide)
thin cardboard
a KnowHow circle maker (see page 5)
strong glue and scissors
paint and a paint brush
20 draught counters

Make a KnowHow circle maker (see page 5). Punch a hole above the 0 cm mark, 10 cm mark, 20 cm mark and the 30 cm mark, like this.

Find the middle (see page 5) of the square sheet of cardboard. Draw three circles, like this, using the 10 cm, 20 cm and 30 cm holes of the circle maker.

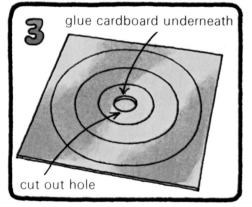

Cut a hole, a bit bigger than a draught counter, out of the centre of the board. Glue a square of card underneath the hole. Then paint the circles different colours.

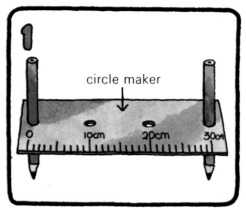

Cut out eight bits of cardboard, each about 8 cm × 3 cm. Make cuts along one edge of each bit (a). Roll them into posts (b). Glue the ends and bend out the cuts (c).

Glue the posts, at equal distances, round the edge of the inside circle, like this. The space between two posts should be big enough for a draught counter to go through.

How to Play

When two people play, each has 10 counters. If four play, in teams of two, each has 5. Partners use the same colour and sit opposite each other.

Take turns to flick the counters, one by one. Try to get them on to the high scoring circles. If a counter lands on a line, count the lower score. Try to flick them behind posts to stop being hit. The player or team with the highest score after all 20 counters have been flicked wins.

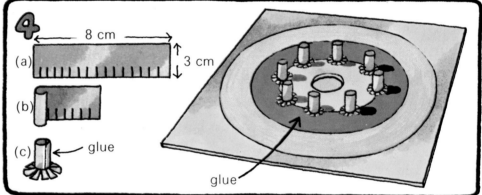

= 5 (outer circle)

= 10 (middle circle)

= 15 (inner circle)

= 25 (hole)

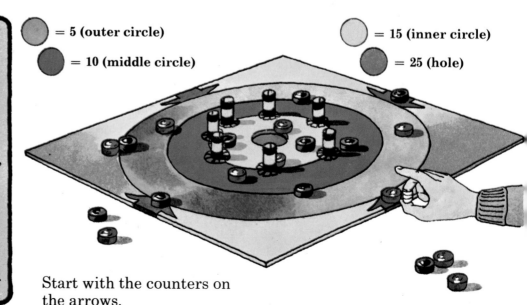

Start with the counters on the arrows.

Jumpers

(for 2 or more players)

This is a different sort of tiddly winks. Try using small, very flat buttons instead of tiddly wink counters

You will need
a cardboard box (about 28 cm long, 22 cm wide and 2 cm deep)
a KnowHow circle maker (see page 5)
a cardboard yoghurt pot
a ruler, a pencil and paint
strong glue and scissors
one big, flat button and 5 tiddly wink counters or small, flat buttons for each player

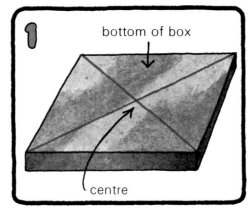

1

bottom of box

centre

Find the centre of the box by ruling lines across it from the four corners, like this. The centre is where the lines cross.

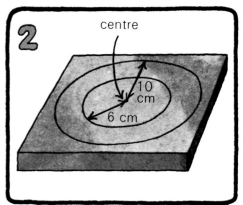

2

centre

10 cm

6 cm

Draw a circle on the box, using the 10 cm hole of the circle maker. Draw a smaller circle, using a hole punched above the 6 cm mark on the circle maker, like this.

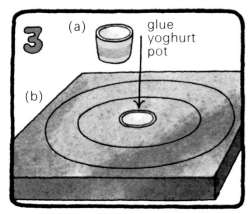

3

(a) glue yoghurt pot

(b)

Cut the top off a yoghurt pot so it is as deep as the box (a). Put the bottom of the pot in the centre of the box. Draw round it. Cut out the circle. Glue pot inside the hole (b).

4

Draw ten lines across the outside and inside circles to make ten sections, like this. Paint the sections different colours.

How to Play

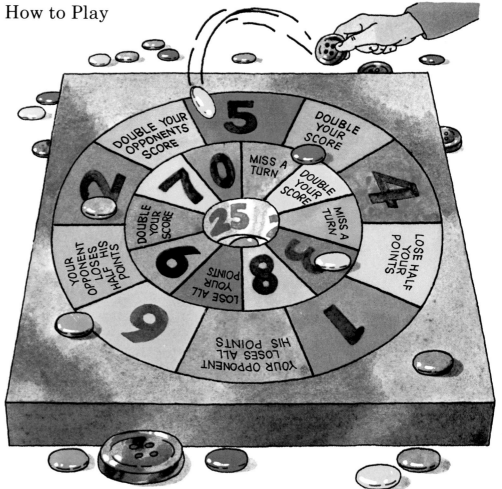

DOUBLE YOUR OPPONENTS SCORE

5

DOUBLE YOUR SCORE

MISS A TURN

DOUBLE YOUR SCORE

2

7

0

MISS A TURN

4

25

DOUBLE YOUR SCORE

6

8

LOSE ALL YOUR POINTS

LOSE HALF YOUR POINTS

YOUR OPPONENT LOSES HALF HIS POINTS

1

9

YOUR OPPONENT LOSES ALL HIS POINTS

Draw the numbers and words inside the sections. Each player has a big, flat button and five small tiddly winks. Players sit opposite each other, about 1 metre from the board.

Taking it in turns, use the button to make the tiddly winks jump on to the board. The player with the highest score after all the tiddly winks have been jumped is the winner.

29

Skittle Scatter

(for 2 or more players)

You will need

8 cardboard tubes (each about 7 cm long)

a strong cardboard box without a lid (about 34 cm wide and 38 cm long)

a smaller box (about 30 cm wide and 32 cm long)

thin cardboard, coloured paper and silver foil

a big plate, a knitting needle, a hairpin and a cotton reel

dowelling (about 45 cm long) or a thin stick

strong glue and some string

a pencil, ruler and scissors

paint and a paint brush

1 Making the Skittles

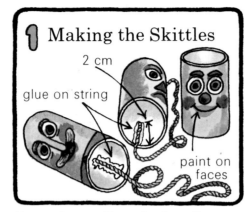

Paint the cardboard tubes. Leave them to dry. Paint on faces. Cut eight pieces of string, each about 80 cm long. Glue one end of each piece to the inside of each tube.

2

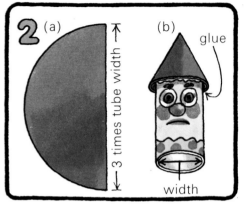

To make cone hats, cut out half-circles of thin cardboard at least three times as wide as the tubes (a). Roll them into cones and glue them on to the tubes (b).

3

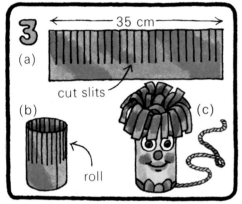

To make hair, cut slits in strips of thin paper about 35 cm long (a). Roll the paper up (b). Push a rolled strip into a cardboard tube and bend over the strips, like this (c).

4

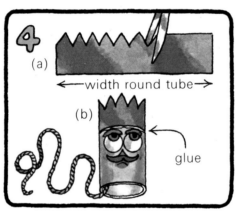

To make crowns, cut strips of thin cardboard, long enough to wrap round the tubes. Cut triangles on one edge of each strip (a). Wrap a strip round a tube and glue it (b).

5 Making the Base

Draw a circle on the bottom of the big cardboard box, close to one corner, using a big plate as a guide, like this.

6

Put strong glue round the edges of the smaller box. Glue it, bottom end up, to the inside of the big box, underneath the circle you have drawn. Leave it to stick.

7

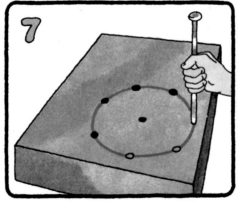

Using a long knitting needle, make seven holes round the outside of the circle and one in the middle. Make sure the needle goes through the box glued under the circle.

8

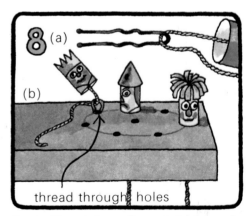

Loop the string of one tube round a hairpin (a). Push it through one of the holes and pull it out of the same hole in the box underneath (b). Do the same to all the tubes.

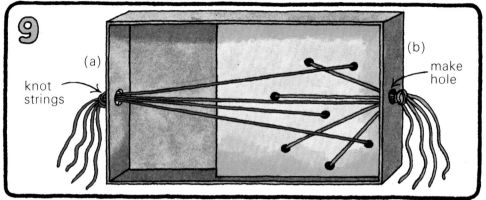

9 Make a hole at both ends of the big box. Thread the four strings furthest away from end **(a)** through that hole. Thread the other four strings through end **(b)**, like this.

Pull all the strings, like this. Knot the four strings at either end together. When you pull the strings the skittles that have fallen over will stand up.

10 The Skittle Hitter

To make the skittle hitter, glue a cotton reel to the corner of the box. Wrap silver foil round the bottom of the stick and push it into the hole in the reel. Tie some string to the top of the stick. Tie a marble, wrapped in foil, to the other end, so it hangs just above the box, like this.

How to Play

Pull the strings to make all the skittles stand up. Swing the skittle hitter and try to knock over as many skittles as you can. Pull them up again. Each player has two swings in a turn. The first one to knock over 20 skittles is the winner.

Another way to play is to paint numbers, from 1 to 8, inside the skittles. To score, add up the numbers inside fallen skittles. The first to score 50 wins.

Cops and Robbers

(for 2 or 4 players)

This is a hunt through a maze. One player or team has six cops, the other has six robbers.

You will need
cardboard (about 45 cm long and 45 cm wide)
thin cardboard and tracing paper
plasticine
2 yoghurt pots
2 big buttons
thin elastic or thin rubber bands
white paper and strong glue
a pencil and a ruler
a red crayon and paint

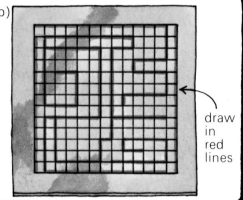

Draw a square, 39 cm long and 39 cm wide, on the thick cardboard. Draw marks every 3 cm along the four sides of the square, like this (a).

Rule lines from the top marks to the bottom marks and from side to side to make small squares. Draw in the red lines as shown (b).

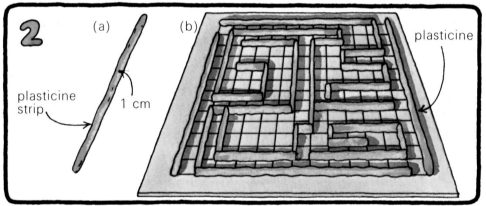

To make the hedges, roll bits of plasticine into long strips, each about 1 cm wide (a). Put the strips along the red lines drawn on the cardboard.

Push the plasticine strips down gently so that they stick to the cardboard. Then pinch the plasticine until the strips are about 2 cm high, like this (b).

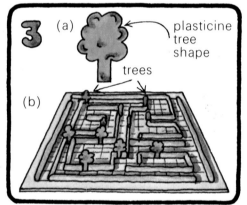

Make eleven plasticine tree shapes (a). Put them on top of the hedges, like this (b). Look at the big picture opposite to make sure you put the trees in the right places.

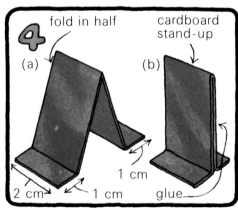

Cut out twelve strips of thin cardboard, each 2 cm wide and 7 cm long. Fold them in half and bend out the ends (a). Glue the two halves together, like this (b).

Draw the cop pattern and the robber pattern (a) on to some tracing paper. Trace the cop pattern on to one side of six of the cardboard stand-ups.

Trace the robber pattern on to one side of the other six cardboard stand-ups. Then paint all the cops and robbers (b).

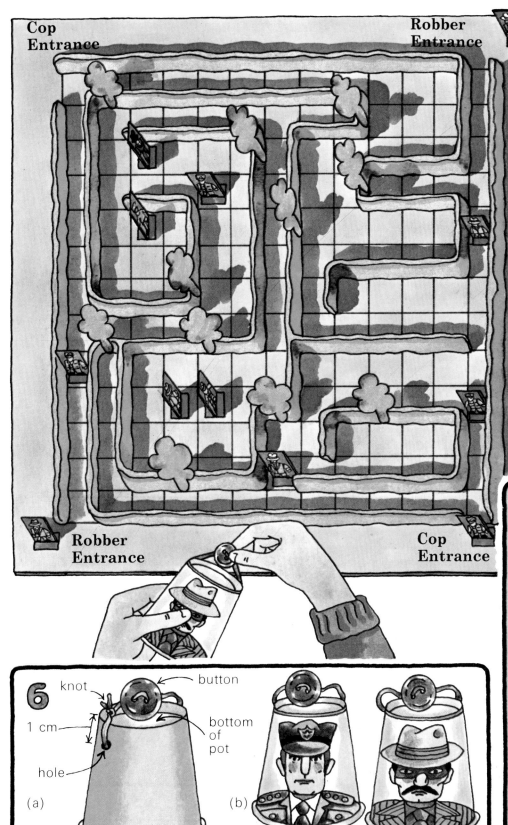

Cop Entrance

Robber Entrance

Robber Entrance

Cop Entrance

6 knot — button

1 cm — bottom of pot

hole —

(a)

(b)

cop gun — robber gun

Make a hole, 1 cm from the base, on either side of the yoghurt pots. Thread thin elastic through the holes and thread a big button on to the elastic. Knot the ends (a).

Cover the yoghurt pots with white paper. Paint a picture of a cop on one of the pots and a picture of a robber on the other pot (b). These are the guns.

How to Play

The idea is to shoot all the other player's men. One player moves the cops and has the cop gun. The other moves the robbers and has the robber gun. If you play in teams of two, each player then moves three men.

To start, put three cops at each of the cop entrances and three robbers at each of the robber entrances. Each player moves one man 5 squares in a turn. They can move in any direction, except diagonally. To shoot an enemy, a player's man must land on the square next to one occupied by an enemy. He then pulls the button on his gun and shouts, 'you are dead'. He takes the man off the board.

Men can only jump over a hedge where there is a tree. They cannot shoot through a hedge except where there is a tree. The first player or team to shoot all enemy men wins.

Picture Puzzles

(for 1 or more players)

Jumble up the Picture Box pieces. See who can put the picture in the right order in the shortest time.

Jumble up the Jigsaw pieces and make up the picture.

Tilt the Heads and Tails to get the balls into the holes. Shake it to get the rings on the pins.

For Picture Box you will need

a small, strong cardboard box
thin and thick cardboard
a picture or photograph
sticky tape and strong glue
scissors, a pencil and a ruler

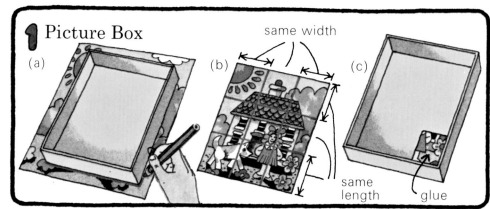

1 Picture Box

same width

same length

glue

Put the box on to a picture or photograph and draw round it (a). Cut the shape out, making it $\frac{1}{2}$ cm smaller all the way round. Divide the length and width into three.

Rule lines across and down to make nine equal pieces, like this (b). Cut out the piece in the bottom right hand corner and glue it inside the box, as shown (c).

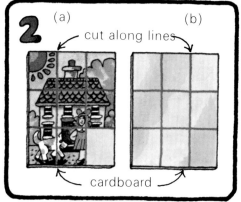

2 (a) (b)

cut along lines

cardboard

Cut two bits of thin cardboard the size of the picture. Glue the picture to one bit (a) and cut along the lines. Divide the other bit into nine pieces (b). Cut along the lines.

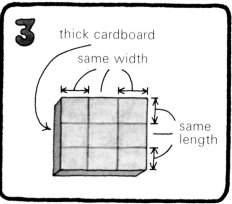

3 thick cardboard

same width

same length

Cut a piece of thick cardboard half as big as the bottom of the box. Measure and rule lines across and down it to make nine equal pieces, like this. Cut along the lines.

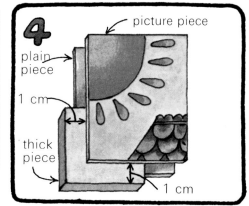

4 picture piece

plain piece

1 cm

thick piece

1 cm

Glue a piece of thick cardboard in between a plain and a pictured piece, like this. The thick piece should stick out about 1 cm from the left hand corner.

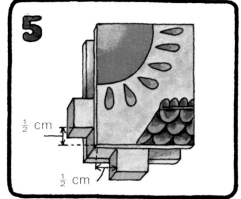

5

$\frac{1}{2}$ cm

$\frac{1}{2}$ cm

Wait until the glue has dried on all eight sandwiched pieces. Then, using scissors, cut all the thick pieces into this shape.

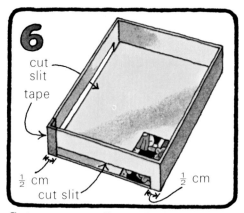

6 cut slit

tape

$\frac{1}{2}$ cm

cut slit

$\frac{1}{2}$ cm

Cut a narrow slit on the bottom left side of the box and the front end, like this, without cutting through the corner. Put sticky tape over the corner, like this.

7

Put the picture into the right order. Then put the pieces into the box, like this, so that the thick bits of cardboard slide inside the picture pieces on either side.

You will need

scissors, strong glue, a pencil
a ruler, paint or crayons

For the Jigsaw

thick cardboard
a picture or photograph

For the Heads and Tails

a round, deep cardboard cheese
    box with a lid
thin cardboard
3 cake decoration balls
a knitting needle
4 drawing pins
4 small curtain rings
cellophane
2 pictures or photographs

1 Jigsaw

Glue a picture on to some thick cardboard. Cut the cardboard in half in wriggly lines from top to bottom and from side to side, like this.

2

Cut the pieces in half again in wriggly lines. Go on cutting the pieces until you have lots of little pieces. Jumble them about and then make up the picture again.

1 Heads and Tails

Draw two circles on some cardboard, using the bottom and the lid of the round cheese box. Cut the circles out, making them a little smaller all the way round.

2

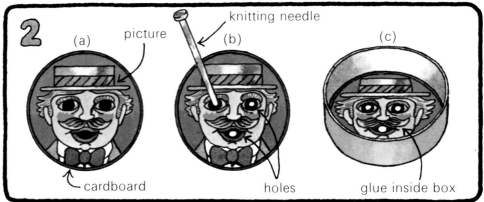

Glue a picture or photograph to one circle (a). Make three holes in the picture using a knitting needle (b). Make sure the holes are clear of any cardboard bits.

See in which one it fits, and then glue the picture inside either the lid or the bottom of the cheese box, like this (c).

3

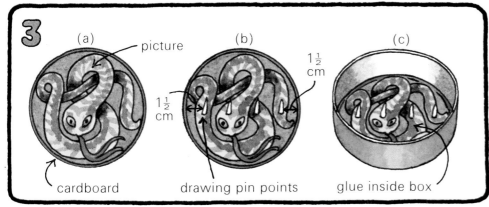

Glue a picture or photograph to the other cardboard circle (a). Push four drawing pins through the picture, like this (b), making sure they are not too close to the edges.

Glue the picture inside the other part of the cheese box, like this (c). Leave it to dry.

4

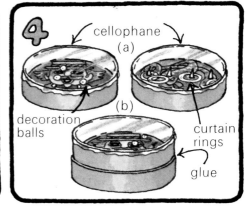

Put the rings into the box with the drawing pins and the balls into the other box. Glue cellophane to the tops of both boxes (a). When they dry, glue the lid to the bottom (b).

Shotpot

(for 2 or more players)

This is a shooting gallery. Try to shoot the buttons or beads out of the pots and down the ramp.

You will need
a cardboard box with a lid
   (about 32 cm × 16 cm)
6 yoghurt pots of the same size
a sheet of cardboard
a piece of cloth
thick paper
a cannon (see page 17)
6 marbles and some beads or
   buttons
strong glue and sticky tape
a pencil and some scissors

Draw six circles inside the bottom of the cardboard box, using the top of a yoghurt pot as a guide. Cut out the circles, making them a little smaller all the way round.

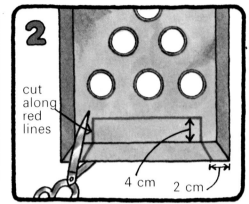

Make an opening, about 4 cm high and 2 cm from each side, in one end of the cardboard box bottom. Cut along the red lines as shown.

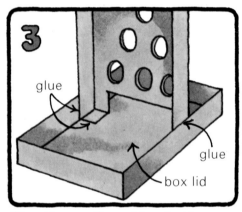

Glue the cardboard box bottom about two-thirds of the way down the inside of the lid, like this.

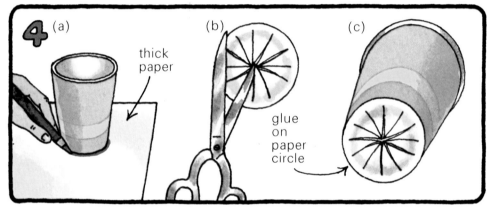

Draw six circles on thick paper, using the top of a yoghurt pot. Cut the circles out (a). Make a hole in the middle of each paper circle, using closed scissors.

Cut 12 slits from the hole to about ½ cm from the edge of each paper circle, like this (b). Glue one paper circle to the top of each yoghurt pot (c). Leave to dry.

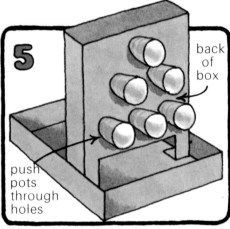

Cut out the bottom of each yoghurt pot. Push the pots, top end first, through the holes in the box, like this. The rims should just stick out on the other side.

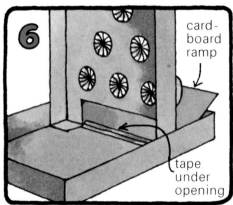

Cut a strip of cardboard as wide as the inside of the box lid and about one-third of the length. Rest it on the back of the lid and tape it under the opening, like this.

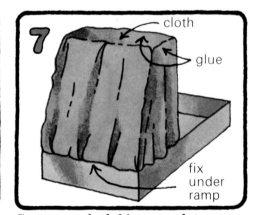

Cut some cloth big enough to cover the back and sides of the upright box. Glue one end of the cloth to the top of the box. Put the other end under the cardboard ramp.

How to Play

Lift up the cloth and put three beads or buttons inside each yoghurt pot. Fix the cloth under the ramp. Fire marbles from the cannon and try to knock the beads out of the yoghurt pots, so they slide down the ramp and through the opening.

Each player fires six marbles in a turn. Each bead counts as one point. Add up the points after each turn. The first player to knock 20 beads through the opening wins.

glue on strip

cut open flap

Cut open the end of the box lid and push it down flat. Cut two strips of cardboard the same length as the lid and as high.

Cut slits, about 1 cm long, in one end of each cardboard strip. Bend the slits forward and glue them to the sides of the lid, like this.

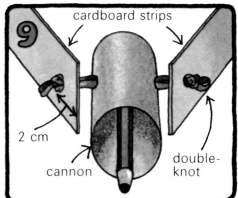

cardboard strips

2 cm

cannon

double-knot

Make a cannon (see page 17). Make a hole in both the cardboard strips, about 2 cm from the ends. Push the two rubber bands through the holes and double-knot the ends.

Floor War

(for 2 players or 2 teams)

You will need

an old sheet or cheap material
(about 2 metres × 2 metres)
4 drawing pins
tracing paper and white paper
thin cardboard and thin twigs
4 cotton reels, 4 plastic cartons
and 4 cardboard egg boxes
4 empty matchboxes, 4 short
pencils and thick cardboard
strong rubber bands and lots of
strips of paper
a ruler, a felt pen and a pencil
scissors and paint
(You can also mark out the
squares of the battlefield with
chalk on any hard floor.)

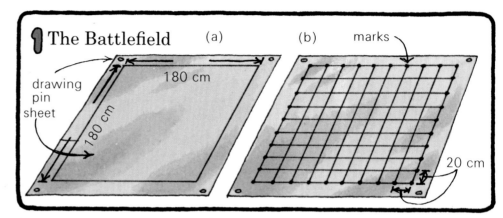

1 The Battlefield

Pin the sheet or material to the floor or carpet with drawing pins, like this. Draw a square, 180 cm long and 180 cm wide, on the sheet or material using a felt pen (a).

Draw marks every 20 cm along the sides of the square. Rule lines from the top marks to the bottom marks and from side to side, like this (b).

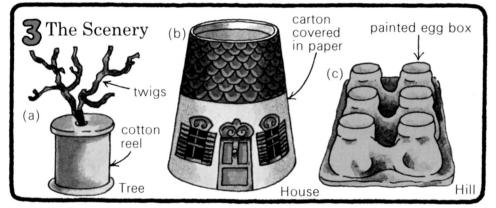

3 The Scenery

To make a tree, push small twigs into the hole in a cotton reel (a). Wrap and glue paper round a tall carton and paint it, like this, to make a house (b).

Cut an egg box in half. Paint the half with egg holders, like this, to make hills (c). Make four trees, four houses and four sets of hills.

4 Model Gun

To make a model gun, glue a small pencil or stick to the top of a matchbox, like this. Glue two small cardboard circles to each side. Both teams need two guns.

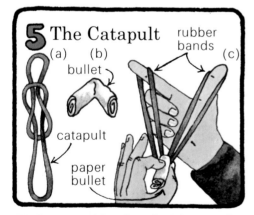

5 The Catapult

Link two rubber bands (a) to make a catapult. Make paper bullets, as shown (b). To fire, put a bullet round the bands (c). Aim, pull back the bullet and then let it go.

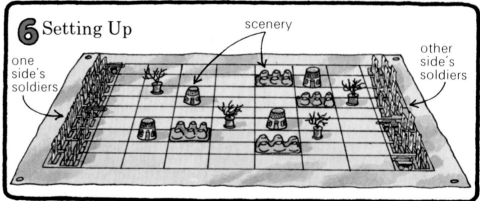

6 Setting Up

One side first lays out the scenery in any way they like in the squares on the battlefield. The other side then chooses which edge they will enter the field from.

The first side then enters from the opposite edge. Each team sets up its soldiers and guns in the first row of squares at their edge of the battlefield, like this.

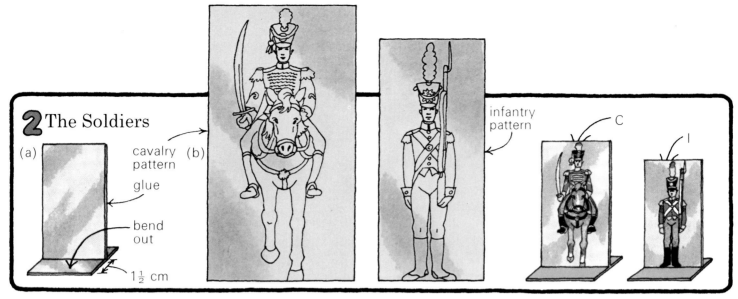

2 The Soldiers

(a)

cavalry pattern (b)

glue

bend out

1½ cm

infantry pattern

C

I

Cut out 20 strips of thin cardboard, each about 18 cm long and 4 cm wide. Then cut out 40 smaller strips, each about 16 cm long and 3 cm wide. Fold the strips in half.

Bend out the ends, like this. Glue the two halves together (a). Trace the cavalry pattern on the 20 big stand-ups and the infantry pattern on the 40 smaller ones (b).

Draw a C on the back of the cavalry stand-ups and an I on the back of the infantry ones. Each team has 10 cavalry and 20 infantry. Paint each team's soldiers a different colour (c).

PLAYERS MUST BE ON THE EDGE OF BATTLEFIELD WHEN FIRING

CATAPULT

EXTRA BULLETS

DEAD SOLDIERS

PAPER BULLET

DEAD CAVALRY

SOLDIERS HIDING BEHIND HILL

DEAD TREE

KILLING OFF GUN ESCORT TO PREVENT GUN FROM FIRING

GUN HIDDEN BEHIND TREE

CAVALRY GUARDING GUN

SOLDIERS KILLING EACH OTHER

How to Play

The game is to kill all enemy soldiers. Each side has a catapult. Toss a coin to see which side starts. Both sides may move all their soldiers in a turn. Infantry, cavalry and guns can move in any direction except diagonally. Cavalry can move up to 3 squares in a turn. Infantry and guns only 1. Cavalry and guns cannot go into squares with scenery.

You must have 4 infantry in the same square as a gun for it to be allowed to move or fire. A gun can either move or fire once in a turn. When a gun is within 6 squares of any enemy soldiers, use your catapult and paper bullets to knock them over. Fire from your side of the field over the model gun you are pretending to fire.

Take any soldiers knocked over by catapult fire off the field. As many soldiers as you like can occupy the same square, but the more there are the easier they will be to hit. Any soldiers put into the same square as enemy soldiers, kill the same number of enemy soldiers, but also are killed themselves. The first side to kill all the enemy soldiers wins.

Space Mission

(for 2 or 3 players)

Play the game on this space board. There are twelve Galaxies, each with five stars.

You will need
3 red, 3 blue, 3 green spaceships
  (made as shown below)
1 white, 1 blue, 1 red dice

How to Play

A player has three spaceships of one colour, each with a white, blue or red flag. He moves his ships from Start to Finish, going from 1 Galaxy to 12 Galaxy in order. Each turn a player throws the three dice. He moves his ship with the white flag the number on the white dice, the blue one for the blue dice and the red one for the red dice. Ships go in any direction along the lines, moving one red dot or star for each point on a dice. A player must have one ship on a Galaxy star before his other two can move to the next Galaxy. If a player throws the same number on all three dice, he has another turn. No ship can land twice on a dot or star in a turn. No ship can land on the same dot as another ship, or jump over a ship.

How to Score

Mark down your score after each turn. When a player's ship lands on a Galaxy star, it scores 1 point. If his second ship lands on a star while the first ship is on the same Galaxy, it scores 3 points. If his third ship lands on the same Galaxy, it scores 5 points.
The game ends when one player gets his three ships to Finish. Each ship scores 3 points when it reaches Finish. The player with the most points at the end of the game wins.

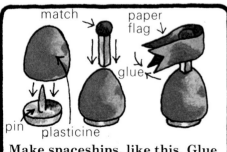

Make spaceships, like this. Glue on white, red or blue paper flags.

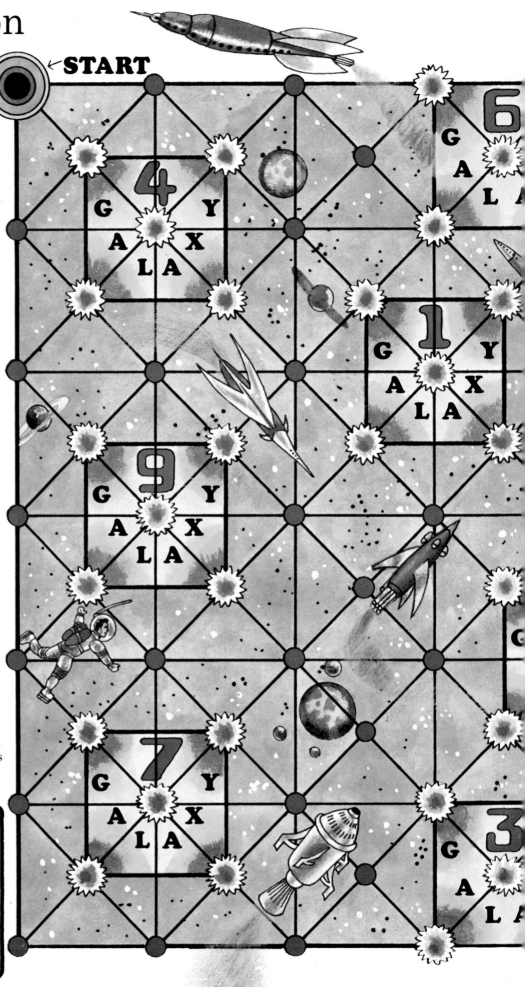

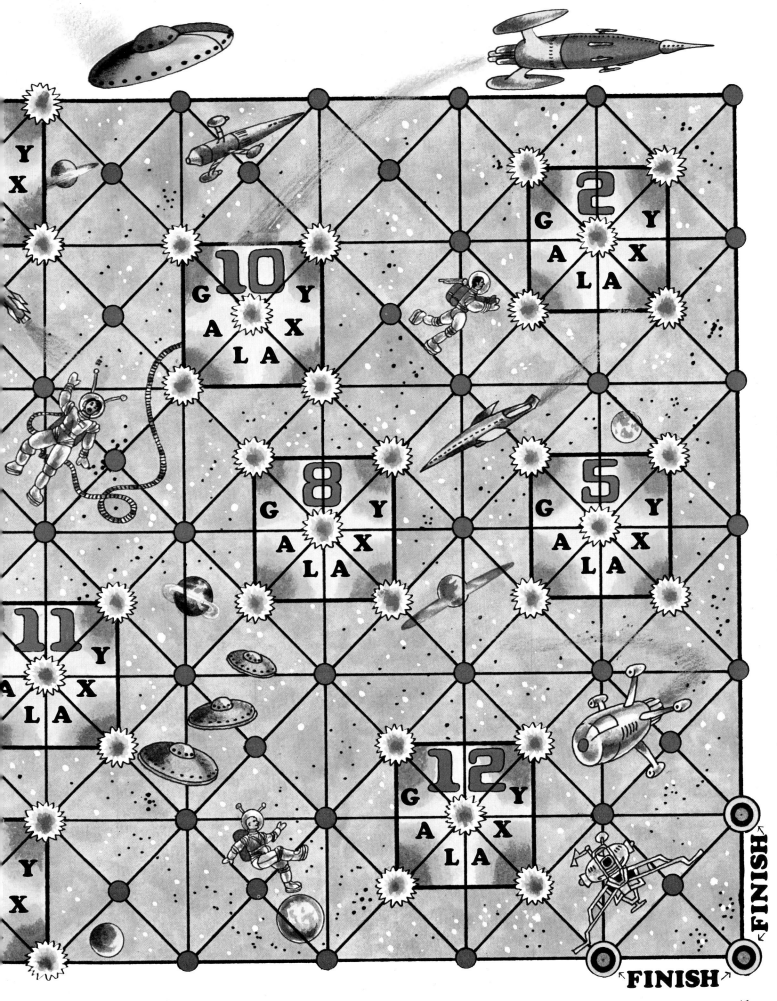

41

Party Games
(for lots of players)

Cotton Balls

Put two bowls beside each other on the floor. Fill one with cotton wool balls. Each player is blindfolded in turn and given a big spoon.

The idea is to scoop up the balls with the spoon and drop them into the empty bowl. Each player has three tries and scores 2 points for each ball he gets into the second bowl. The player with the most points at the end wins.

Murder in the Dark

Cut out as many slips of paper as there are players. Mark an X on one and a D on another. Leave the rest blank. Fold them in half and give one to each player. The player with the slip marked X is the murderer. He keeps it secret. D is the detective. He tells everyone.

The lights are put out and everybody hides except the detective. The murderer creeps up on a hidden player, whispers 'you are dead' and runs off. The victim screams, the lights go on and everyone gathers round him. The detective asks questions to find out who the murderer is. Only the murderer can lie. The detective has 3 guesses to find the murderer.

Parcel Dressing Up

Wrap a bar of chocolate in layers of paper tied in string. Players sit in a circle with a hat, a scarf, gloves, glasses, a knife and a fork in the middle. They take turns to throw a dice. When someone throws a 6, he takes the clothes from the middle, puts them on and tries to open the parcel with the knife and fork.

The others go on throwing the dice. When one throws a 6, he pulls the clothes off the first person, puts them on and opens the parcel with the knife and fork. This goes on until the parcel has been opened and all the chocolate squares have been eaten.

The Posting Game

Hide ten tins, each with the name of a city written on it, round the house. Each player gets a box with ten slips of folded paper in it. On each slip is written the name of one of the cities. All the boxes are put in one room.

Each player takes one slip at a time, writes his name on the back and rushes round the house to find the tin with the same name as his slip. When he finds it, he posts the slip in the tin and goes back for his next slip. The first player to post all ten slips in the right tins is the winner.

Whisper Story

Everyone sits in a line. The player at one end makes up a long story and whispers it to the person beside him. The second player then whispers the story to the next person. This goes on down the line until the last person has heard the story. He tells it out loud. Then the first person tells the real story.

Sardines

One player hides somewhere in the house. He must hide in a place big enough to hold more people. The other players count to 50 and then go off to look for him. Anyone who finds him quietly joins him in the hiding place. The last person to find him has to pay a forfeit.

Eaties

Everybody is blindfolded. A plate with ten different bits of food on it is put in front of each player. They taste the food. The plates are taken away and the blindfolds taken off. The players write down what they think they have eaten. Put things like cold peas and cold porridge on each plate.

Stop Game

Play this game while everyone is eating. First choose a 'stop' caller. Everybody starts eating. Suddenly the caller shouts 'stop' and everyone has to freeze. No one can eat or move, except the 'stop' caller until he calls 'move on'. Everyone has a go at being the 'stop' caller.

Spin the Bottle

Put a bottle on a table and all sit round the table. One player spins the bottle. Whoever it points to when it stops spinning has to pay a forfeit. Think up lots of forfeits before you begin, such as eating an apple without bending your elbows or chewing half a lemon.

Party Races

(for lots of players)

Stepping Stone Tins

Each player has two tins. They race each other from one end of the room to the other using their tins as stepping stones.

To start, stand on one foot on one tin. Then bend down and, without touching the floor, put the second tin in front of the first. Step on it with your other foot. Then bend down and put the first tin in front. Do this again and again until you get to the other end of the room

Flower Pot Stilts

To make a flower pot stilt, make a hole on each side of a plastic flower pot, near the base. Pull string through the holes and knot the ends.

Players split into two teams. Each team has two stilts. They stand at one end of the room with two chairs at the other. The first player in each team stands on the stilts, holds the string, walks round the chair and back and gives the stilts to the next player. The first team to get round the chair and back wins.

Orange Under the Chin

Two teams stand in two lines. The first player in each team puts an orange under his chin.

The game is to pass the orange from chin to chin down your line without touching it with your hands. If a player drops or touches it, the orange must go back to the beginning of his line. The first team to get its orange to the end of the line wins.

Peas and Straws

Each player has a straw, 30 dried peas in a cup and an empty cup. He puts the cups next to each other on the floor. He has to suck the peas on to the end of his straw and drop them into the empty cup. The first player to get all his peas into the second cup is the winner.

Peas and Pull-Boxes

To make a pull-box, make two holes, about 15 cm apart, in one end of a box. Pull string through the holes and knot the ends.

Players split into two teams and stand at one end of the room with a line of string at the other. Each team has a pull-box with 40 dried peas lined up in front of it. Each member of the team has to pull the box, without losing the peas, to the line and back. The team with the most peas left in front of its box after all the players have pulled it wins.

String Buns

Tie string across a room, about 2 metres from the floor. Cut as many 1 metre bits of string as there are players. Tie one end of each bit to the string across the room. Thread the other end of each bit through a bun. Knot the ends.

Each player has to eat a bun without touching it with his hands. The first to eat his bun wins.

Matchbox Noses

Two teams stand in two lines. The first player in each team puts a matchbox cover on his nose.

The game is to pass the matchbox from nose to nose down your line, without touching it. If a player drops or touches it, the matchbox must go back to the beginning of his line. The first team to get its matchbox to the end of the line wins.

Tissue Fish

Each player gets a rolled up newspaper and a fish shape, cut out of tissue paper. Players split into two teams and stand at one end of the room with two big plates at the other end.

The first player in each team puts his fish on the floor and flaps the newspaper behind it until he gets the fish into his plate. As soon as he does, the next player in his team starts. The first team to get all its fish into its plate wins.

Tissue Squares

Cut out as many squares of tissue paper as there are players. Put two pillows at one end of the room and two plates at the other. Lie half the number of tissue squares on one pillow and half on the other. Players split into two teams. Each team stands next to a plate.

The first player in each team has a spoon. He runs to the pillow, scoops up a tissue square with the spoon, without touching it, and carries it back to his plate. If he drops it, he must scoop it up again without touching it. Once it is on the plate the next player starts. The first team to get all its squares on to its plate wins.

Balloon Bursting

Players split into two teams. They stand at one end of the room. Two chairs, each heaped with as many balloons as there are players in a team, are at the other end.

The first player in each team runs to the chair, blows up a balloon, knots it and sits on it until it bursts. He runs back and touches the next player, who runs to the chair. The first team to blow up and burst all its balloons wins.

Treasure Hunts

(for lots of players)

Arrange the treasure hunts before the party begins. Try not to hide any clues in dangerous places and make sure that even the smallest player can reach them. Tell everyone which rooms are not being used in the hunt.

Players can either hunt by themselves, in pairs or teams.

In a clue-by-clue hunt, try not to let anyone else know that you have found a clue. When you have read it make sure you put it back where you found it.

Camouflage Hunts

Hide 20 small, coloured things, like a red pencil, a yellow button or a green toothbrush, round the house. Hide each thing in or on something of the same colour, perhaps the yellow button on a yellow book or the green toothbrush on a green plate.

Each player gets a list of the hidden things and a pencil and starts looking. When he finds one he writes down its hiding place. The first player to write down the hiding places of all 20 things wins.

Clue-by-Clue Hunts

Write the clues on bits of paper. Hide them round the house, say in a shoe or tap. Each clue tells the players where to find the next clue until they reach the treasure.

Read out the first clue to all the players. In this hunt, the first clue is: 'You'll find clue no. 2 if you put your foot in me'. Now follow the clues to find the treasure.

Hidden Letters

Hide the treasure, say in the bathroom. Write the letters that spell 'bathroom' on different bits of paper. Hide them. Tell everyone how many letters are hidden.

As they find one, the players write down each letter. When a player thinks he knows which room the letters spell, he runs to that room to find the treasure.

THINGS HANG IN ME. I'M OFTEN UNTIDY— SEARCH ME FOR THE TREASURE...

SWITCH ME ON TO FIND THE NEXT *CLUE*...

ANSWER
THE TREASURE IS HIDDEN IN THE CUPBOARD

THE NEXT *CLUE* WILL COME SPLASHING OUT IF YOU TURN ME ON...

Hidden Pictures

Cut some magazine pictures or old Christmas cards in half. Give one half of each picture to a player and hide the other halves round the house.

The first player to find the hidden half of his picture gets a prize. You can make it more difficult by cutting the pictures into quarters and hiding three pieces.

Scavenger Hunts

Each player gets a list of the same ten things to find, perhaps a shoe, a nail, a potato or a hairpin. All the things are somewhere in the house. A player has to collect one of each thing on his list in a certain time, perhaps 15 minutes.

The player who has collected the most things on his list at the end of the time limit is the winner.

Left Standing

Players are shown a small object. They go out of the room. The object is hidden so only a bit of it shows. Everyone comes back into the room and starts looking for it.

When a player sees it he sits down. He does not tell anyone he has seen it or where it is. The last person to see it is left wandering round the room on his own.

47